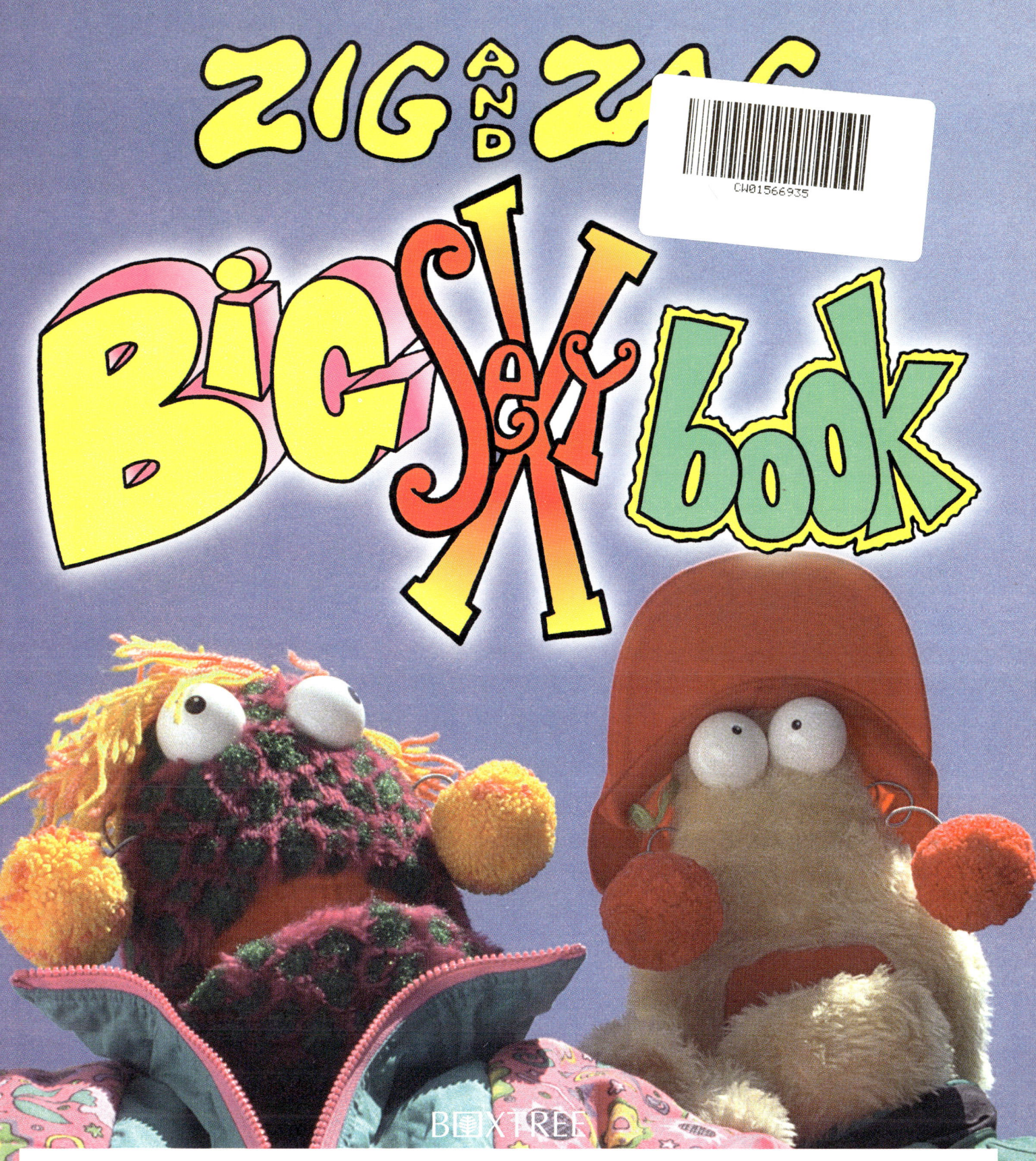

First published in 1994 by Boxtree Limited,
Broadwall House, 21 Broadwall, London SE1 9PL

Copyright © Double Z Enterprises 1994
Licensed by Copyright Promotions Limited

All rights reserved. This publication may not be reproduced, transmitted or held in a retrieval system in part or in whole in any form or using any electronic, mechanical, photocopying or recording process or any other process without the publisher having first given permission in writing.

Except in the United States of America, this book is sold subject to the condition that it shall not, by way of trade or otherwise, be lent, resold, hired out or otherwise circulated without the publisher's prior consent in any form of binding or cover other than that in which it is published and without a similar condition imposed on a subsequent purchaser.

ISBN 0 7522 0860 8

10 9 8 7 6 5 4 3 2 1

NOW AVAILABLE ON EARTH

ZAGACTOL

Spot Right There!

Z57.99

 ✗

 ✓

NO, IT'S NOT A SPELLING MISTAKE. IT'S THE TRUTH!

YOU'VE GOT SPOTS, LOTS OF SPOTS! SO JUST FOR YOU, PIZZA FACE. WE AT Z.A.G. CHEMICALS HAVE DEVELOPED ZAGACTOL - A NEW NAME IN ZIT ZAPPING! MADE FROM PERFECTLY SAFE "PLUTONIOC-PHULSFATE-MONOXIDE-SULPHURIC-FERRIS". IT'S GUARANTEED TO WORK! AND IT'S ALSO GREAT ON GARDENS FOR KEEPING THOSE PESKY WEEDS AT BAY!

We asked top TV personality and chairman of Z.A.G. CHEMICALS, **MR. ZAG** to try out ZAGACTOL for himself.

"IT'S SPOT-TASTICALLY GOOD, MY FACE FEELS SO SMOOTH, AND BOY-OH-BOY, YOU SHOULD SEE MY GARDEN!" BUY IT NOW TEENGERS!!!

Send cheques c/o Z.A.G. Foundation, 10 Zogland Heights, Zog 15, Planet Zog.

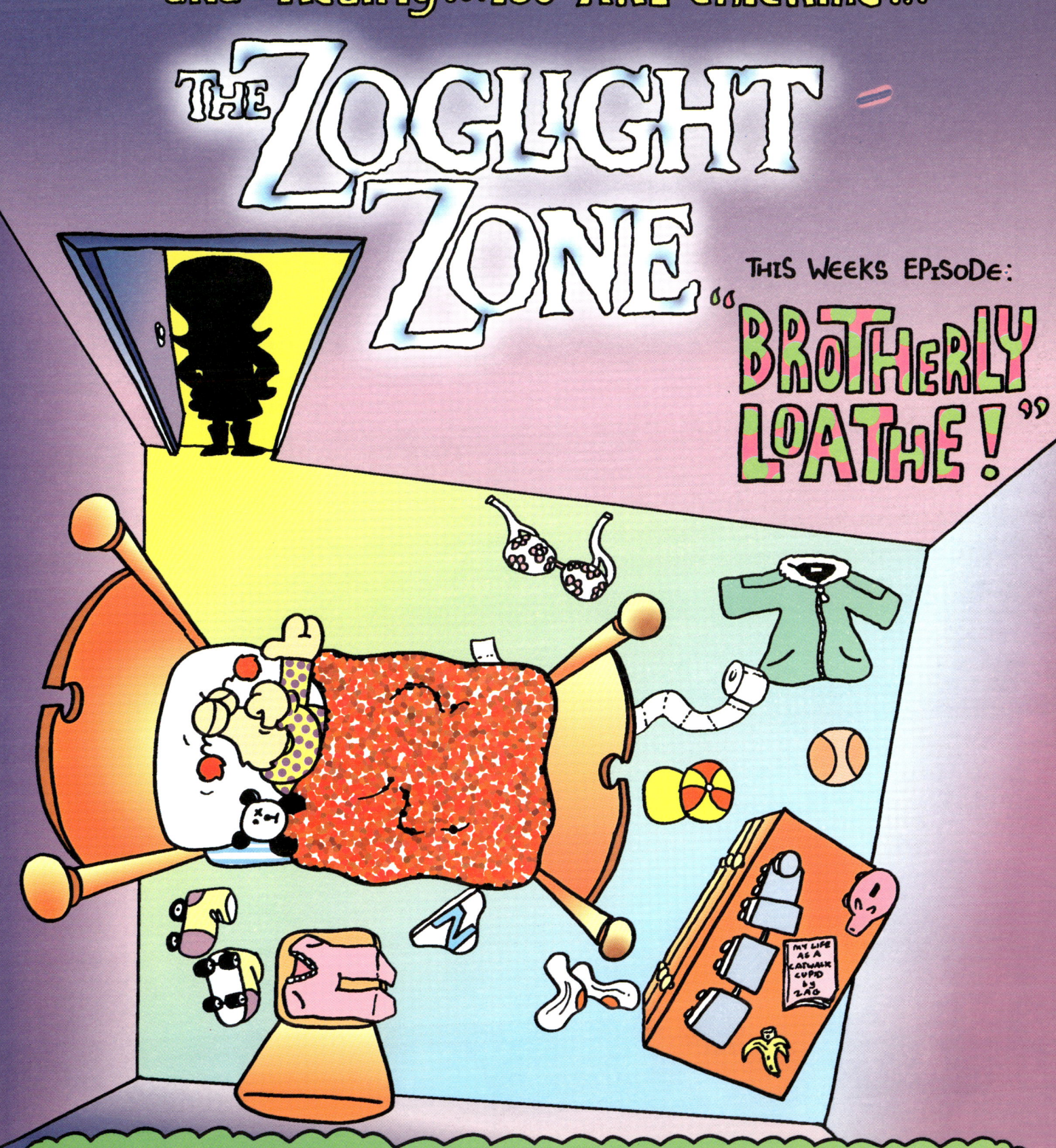

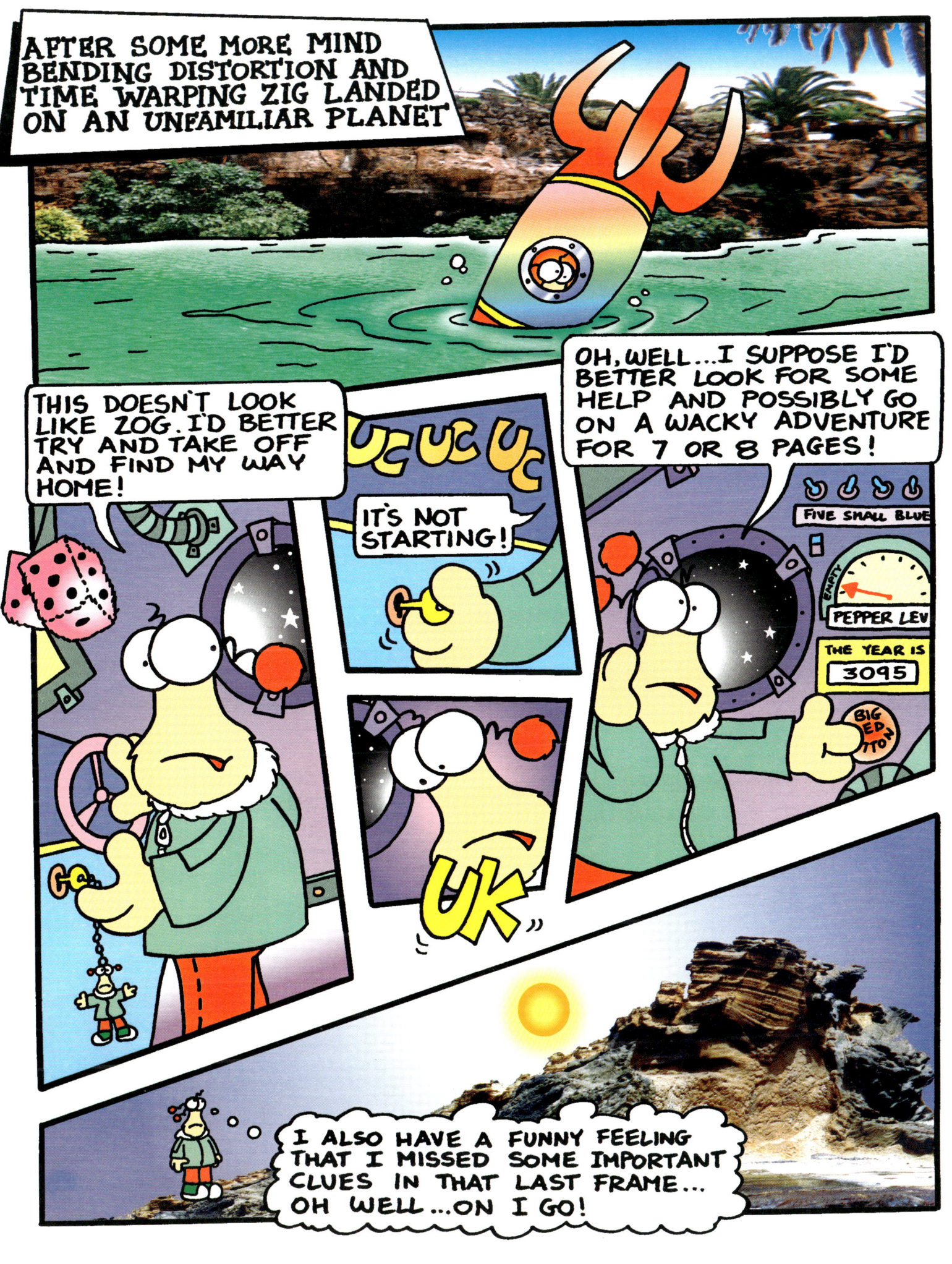

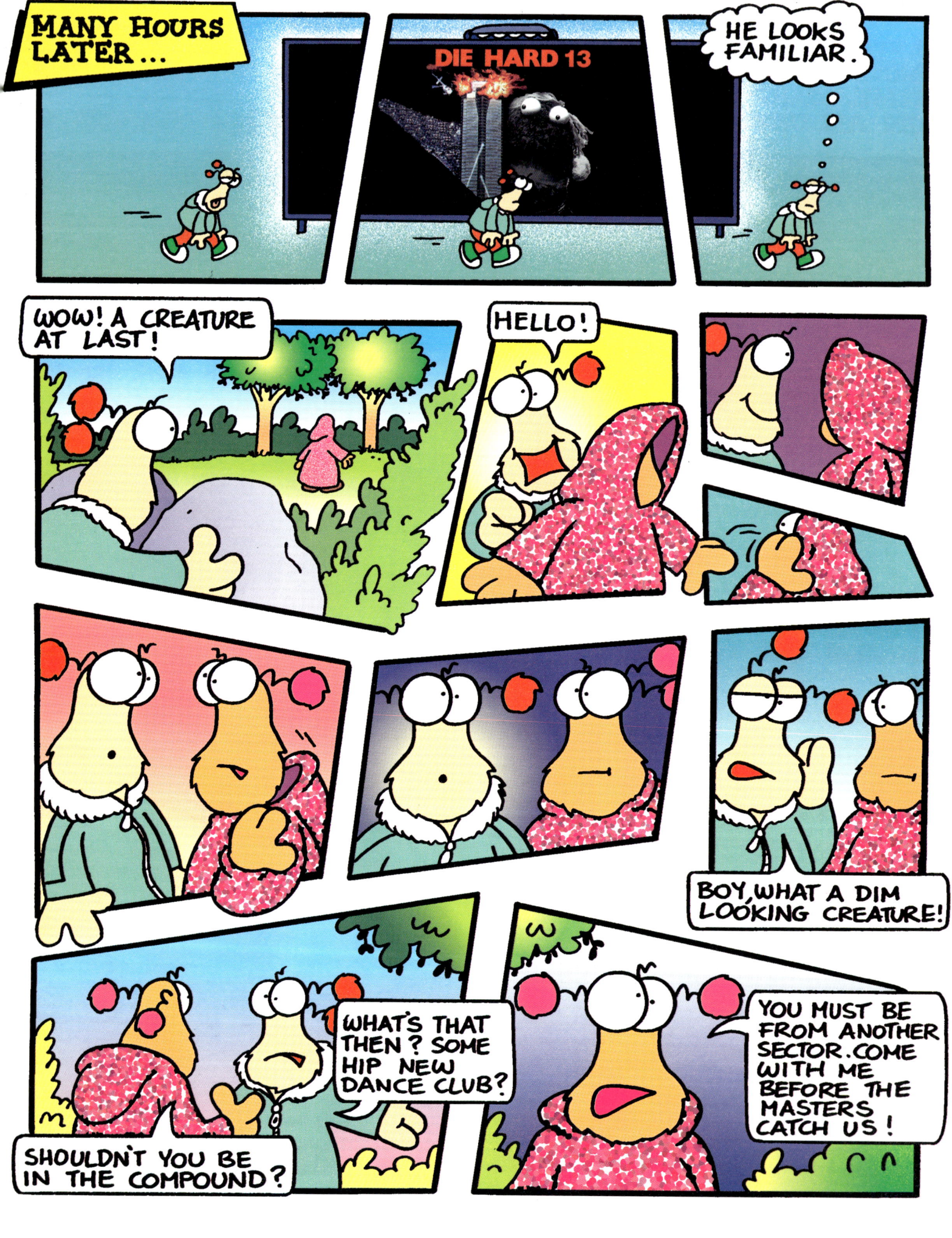

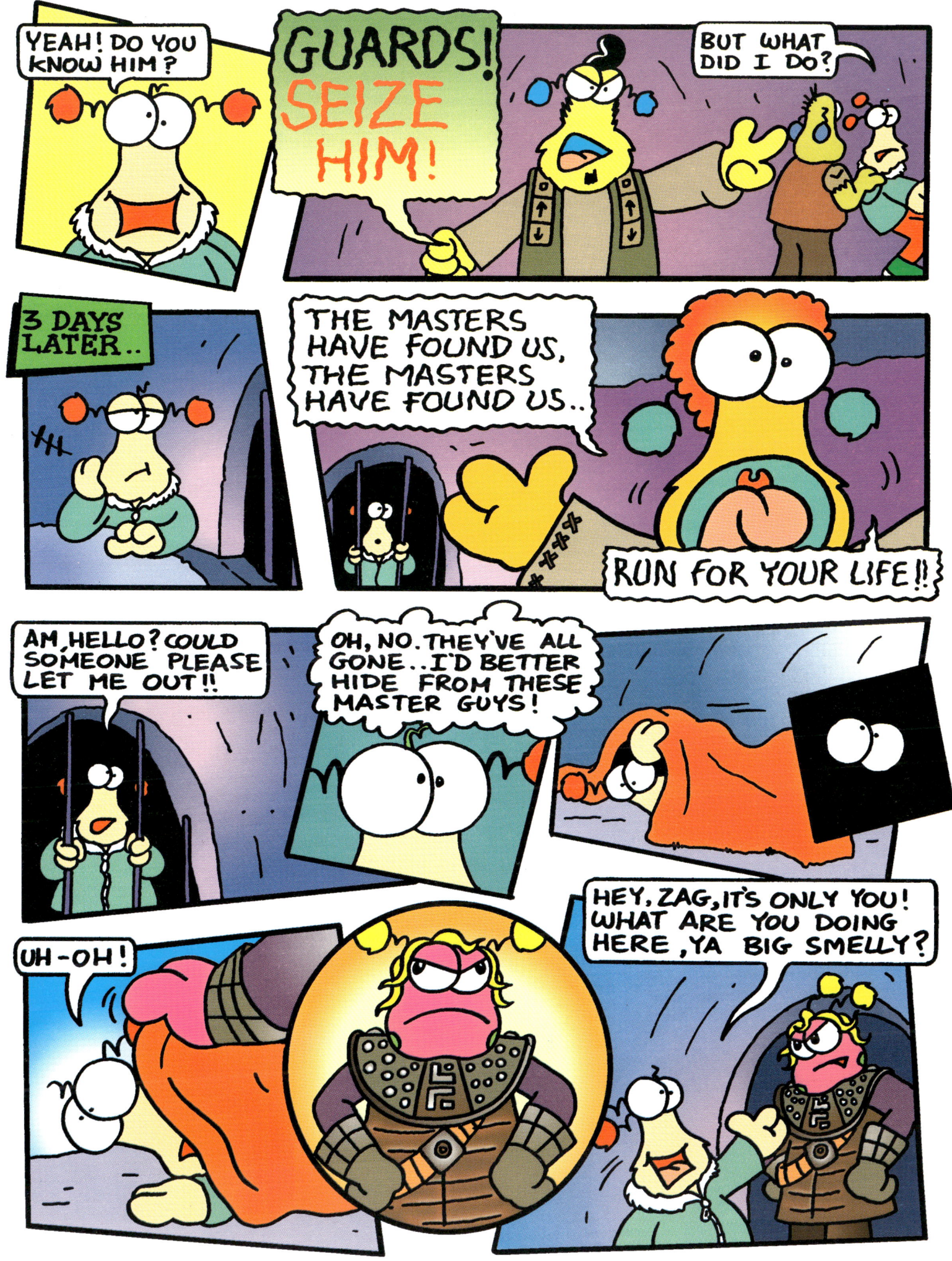

THE 7TH ZOGIAN CHURCH OF FUNK

IS COMING TO YOUR TOWN!

All who shall attend shall be saved from the wrath of soulless easy-listening music by making a large donation to the most funky Grandmaster of the Ghetto-Blaster, Reverend T. Groove!

AVOID A SOUL CRISIS INTERVENTION, JUST BE THERE Y'ALL!

You are now put in a steel bed from the war times and left in a room full of sick people, lucozade and coughing. And each bed has its own shower curtain. Now the girl nurse arrives to give you your medicine. You will know how sick you are by how bad your medicine tastes.
① YUK!
② SUPER YUK!
③ MONKEY PEE!

If you are number ③ you need a nop-eration which will be performed by Chief surgeon, a lady madam nurse, nuns and a kwik-fit-fitter. To find out what is wrong with your insides firstly you must have all your fur shaved off, this is to make pillows for the other ill!

Then the head nurse madam says "COME ON GET YOUR PANTS OFF AND PUT THIS TENT ON AND GET ON WITH IT, THERE'S NOTHING THERE I HAVEN'T SEEN BEFORE!" Then you must HAW! on a silver spoon and if the spoon turns hairy you must go to the theatre very early in the morning.

NURSE, ITS A SAUSAGE!

You must fast from the night before. This makes the night go faster 'cause you don't think about your nop-eration — you think of food and also so the Chief surgeon does not take out a sausage instead of your appendix!

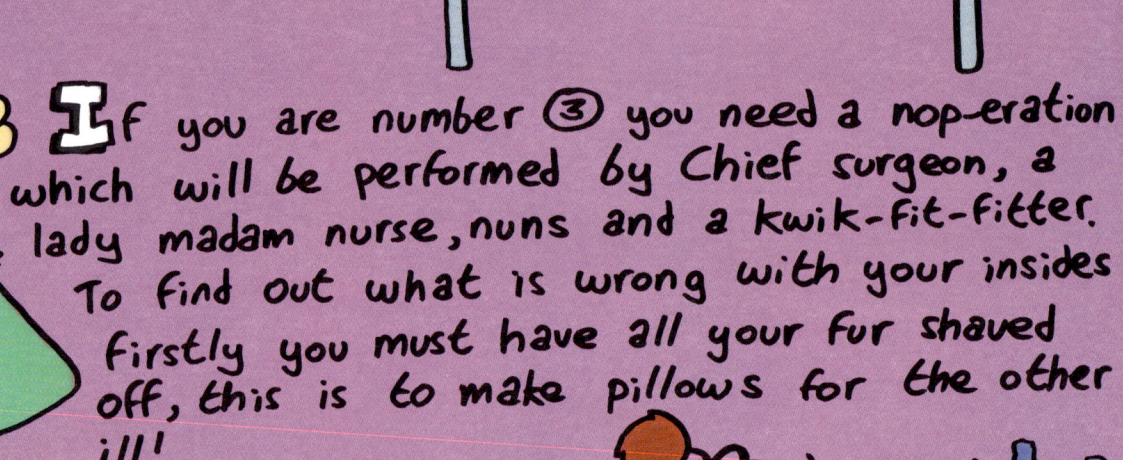

"Now breath deeply," says the man in the gurls outfit. "COUNT TO TEN." Then you get a feeling like you've gone over a hump-backed bridge in a car. Then you are asleep and they play noughts and crosses on your tummy. It is very important that the surgeon wins. After he wins he puts a tiny hole in your belly and looks in with medical binoculars. "THERE'S THE LITTLE RASCAL," he says, "LET'S BE HAVING HIM OUT!"

Then the surgeon uses his magic see-through gloves and grabs the inflection and shouts at the top of his voice "GET OUT AND DON'T COME BACK!" After that the surgeon knits you together again and the lady madam nurse shouts at the nuns, "BOILING WATER! I MUST HAVE BOILING WATER!" Then the kwik-fit-fitter makes you a badge out of an old sheet and water and flour!

After your nop-eration you are kept in hopspital until you are really, really bored. Then you go home and show your sister's friends your scabs!

MR. COCKY and MR. TWIT

In the middle of the woods, miles and miles from anywhere, there was a hill. On one side of the hill lived Mr Cocky and on the other side of the hill lived Mr Twit. Mr Cocky didn't like Mr Twit one single bit.

This story begins one morning when Mr Cocky was woken up by quite a rowdy racket.

"Goodness me, what's that terrible bloomin' noise?" he growled. "I bet it's my lame-brained neighbour, Mr Twit!" Up jumped Mr Cocky out of his bed and told his wife, Miss Supermodel that they must drive their brand new Ford Probe over the hill to Mr Twit's house at once.

"What in the name of Finkle D Farnsworth is going on here?" shouted Mr Cocky in an angry voice.
"No thanks, I already have a hovercraft!" Mr Twit replied in a very silly voice indeed and making no sense whatsoever as usual.
"Oh dear," frowned Miss Supermodel, "they're having a rave."

Why, there's Mr Techno and behind him there's Mr C!"
"Right!" Mr Cocky shouted. "That's enough of that racket!" and as he unplugged the rig he told Mr Twit and his friends that "nobody but nobody was going to ruin his barbecue with that student type malarkey."
"Yo barbecue respect, man," said Mr C "Are we invited man?"

"Indeed not!" grumbled Mr Cocky as he led Miss Supermodel back home to help prepare a light salad with Italian dressing.
At 5 o'clock on the dot Mr Punctual arrived, closely followed by Mr Snotty and Miss Hoity Toity and lashings of other posh guests.

After three hours of Mr Cocky being cocky to his guests even Mr Excitable was bored.
"I know, I shall show you all our plans for our new Gazebo!" said Mr Cocky. "I'll fetch the bloomin' things right now, shall I?" and before anyone could say, "Bog Off," he had dashed indoors.

But when Mr Cocky returned with the plans, all his party guests were gone! This made Mr Cocky furious especially when he heard the techno music from over the hill. "Why, it's that lunatic Mr Twit again, he's scared my friends away!" he fumed.
"As chairman of the residents association I'll send him packing."

So off Mr Cocky stormed to the other side of the hill once more, and lo and behold all his barbecue guests were having a jolly fine time indeed.

"Oh, goodness gracious," he thought as he felt himself move like he'd never moved before. "Oh, gosh, what's happening to me? I appear to be moving in time to this wicked sub bass groove."

"Safe, man," replied Mr C. "Techno, techno, techno!" shouted Mr Techno. "Derek's got a Volvo," replied Mr Twit.

And they all raved until dawn and Mr Cocky hadn't enjoyed himself so much in years, well, that was until Mr.Plop ruined everything when he decided to use Mr Cocky's prize-winning lawn as a loo!

The End!

ZAG'S GLITTERING TV CAREER!

FROM HIS HUMBLE BEGINNINGS AS A STAND-UP COMIC AND FOUNDER MEMBER OF THE SECOND CITY THEATRE GROUP IN CHICAGO, TO HIS LEAD ROLE IN THE 1970'S ROLLER DISCO VERSION OF "FAME," HE HAS SET THE ENTERTAINMENT WORLD ALIGHT. WITH HIS RUGGED LOOKS AND CAPTIVATING PERSONALITY, HE WAS DESTINED TO SIT ON THE THRONE NEXT TO BRANDO. HIS LIFE IS ACTING, HIS NAME IS ZAG!

IN THIS TRIBUTE TO ZAG WE LOOK AT SOME OF THE FINEST MOMENTS OF HIS GLITTERING TV CAREER. ENJOY THE RIDE!

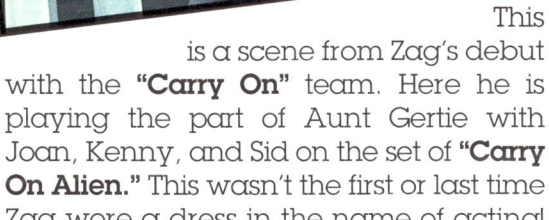

This is a scene from Zag's debut with the **"Carry On"** team. Here he is playing the part of Aunt Gertie with Joan, Kenny, and Sid on the set of **"Carry On Alien."** This wasn't the first or last time Zag wore a dress in the name of acting!

1968 saw Zag in his first leading role. He starred as "Captain Purple" in the "All New Captain Purple Show" alongside Bobby Davro and Cary Grant. **"Captain Purple...he's desirable!"**

In September 1988 a new comedy about four elderly ladies living in Florida was devised by Zag. The show was originally called **"Granny Zag And Her Mates"** and had Zag once again donning a skirt and support tights in the name of comedy. It became an overnight success, but Zag moved on after the second series and out of respect to Zag they changed the programme's name to **"The Golden Girls."**

Zag was approached by the BBC in **1988** to create a **"Neighbours"** type programme in outer space. It was called **"Red Dwarf."** But after only three episodes it became clear that Zag was stealing the limelight from the rest of the cast in his role as **"Blotchy, the Shape-shifter"** and once the first series was completed, he left, having made the decision to let his mate Craig Charles get a few of the laughs.

In **1989** Zag came up with the idea for a programme all about news stories, and along with his showbiz pals Merty and Deaty made a pilot for what was later to become **"Have I got News for You."** Due to another commitment in the U.S. Zag couldn't continue with the full series.

That other commitment was to appear in **"Cheers"** as Sam's niece Betsy-May in the "Cheers" Christmas Special. "Cheers" is filmed in front of a live studio audience in Zag's Coffee Bar in Boston.

"Beverly Hills 90120" fans fondly remember Zag as Johnny Diamond, heart-throb and lead singer in the highschool grunge band **"Strawberry Jam."** The ratings soared, but it all came to an end in his much publicised break-up with his girlfriend and fellow star at that the, Tori "my dad owns the show" Spelling.

1993 saw Zag as Todd Schwartz, the Olympic roller skater-cum-lawyer in the hit show **"LA Law."** His character was hugely popular until his untimely demise in the now legendary and tragic penguin expedition.

It is rumoured that Zag earned over **£300,000,000** for his four guest appearances on British Television's **"London's Burning."** Here we see a rare still from the episode in which he stars as the rogue fire-fighter Quentin Smythe.

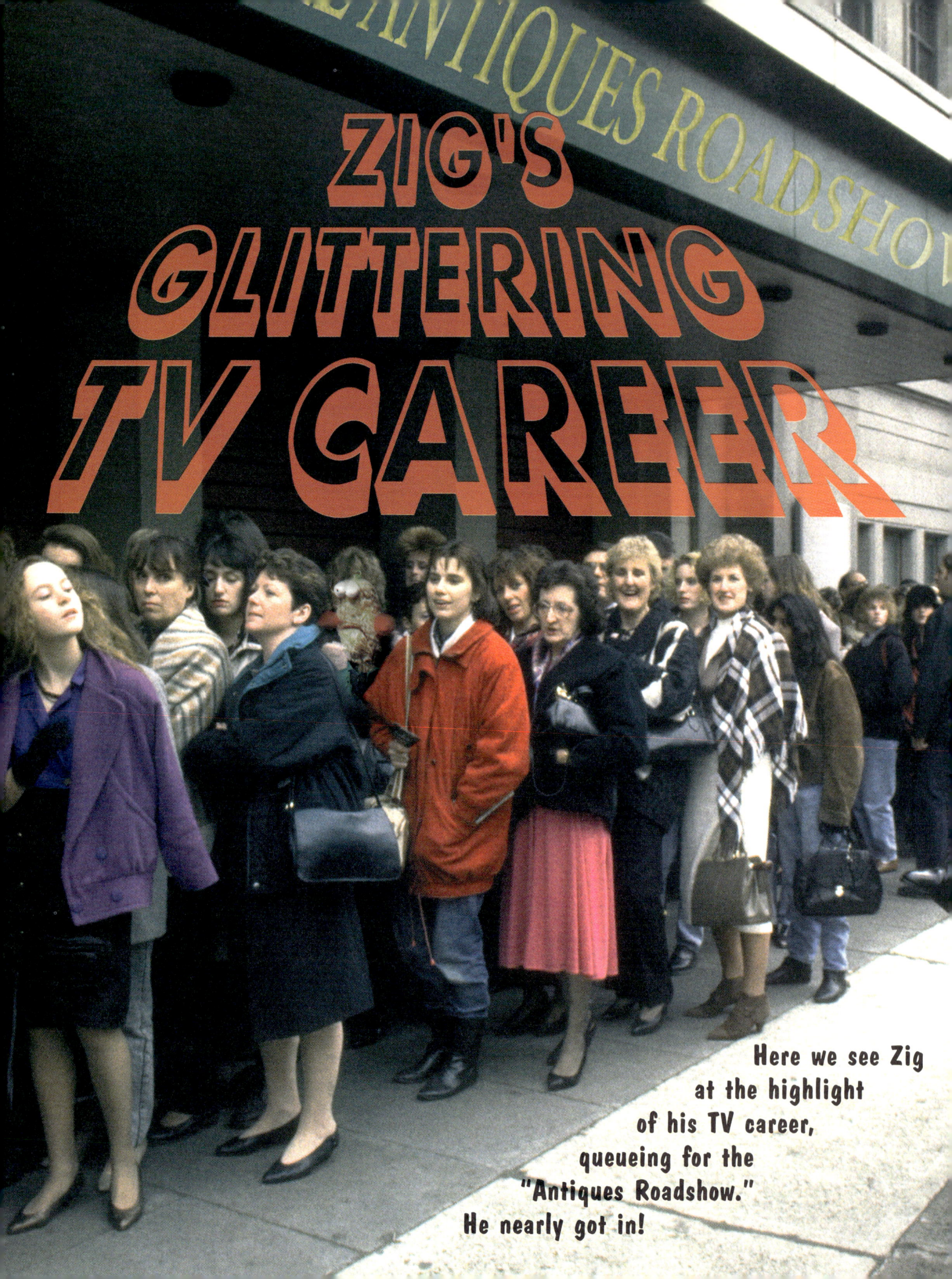

COMING SOON TO A CINEMA NEAR YOU...

Sound Sense From Your Funky Saviour

Dear Rev. Groove,
    I need your help. I'm overwhelmed with guilt. My sister bought the latest "Pet Shop Boys" record and as was my duty laid down by the Ten Funkmandments from the 7th Zogian Book of Funk, I made fun of her for listening to such bland and synthy, over-produced sounds. But despite my efforts she continued to play it every day. After a few weeks I found myself humming to "West End Girls" and I knew all the lyrics off by heart. But it wasn't until the day that I found myself strangely drawn to wearing a traffic cone on my head that I realised the Pet Shop Boys had seeped into my veins and sapped me of all my soul power. I've saved up ₤250 for the Church of Funks Soul Survival Fund, is this enough to buy my soul back?
                  Signed Worried Trevor

OH, LORDY, LORDY! IN THE NAME OF ST. JAMES BROWN, I PRAISE THE LORD THAT YOU HAVE WRITTEN TO ME SINNER. YOUR SOUL MUST BE PURGED OF THESE DEMONS. YOU NEED TO BE FUNKISIZED BROTHER TREV. AND THAT MEANS YOU NEED A SHORT, SHARP, SHOCK... OH LORDY YEEEEESSSS! I AM RECEIVING A HEALING MESSAGE FROM UP ABOVE, YOU GOTTA SEND ME ₤150 MORE, THATS WHAT THE BIG FUNKY ONE IS A TELLING ME....THATS THE PRICE YOU GOTTA PAY TO GET FUNKY ONCE MORE, MY SOUL BROTHER! BUT FOR NOW I WANT YOU TO TOUCH THIS PAGE WHILE YOU WRITE OUT THAT CHEQUE...TOUCH IT NOW BROTHER! NEIL TENNANT... BE GONE! THAT GUY ON THE KEYBOARDS THAT NEVER MOVES OR SAYS A WORD....BE GONE! LET THE HEALING BEGIN!

Sting is cool!
                  Signed Anon.

THIS IS THE WORK OF A DEEEEMON. SOUL BROTHERS AND FUNKY SISTERS, WE GOTTA PRAY NOW. PUT YOUR HANDS ON THE PAGE TO SAVE ANOTHER SOULLESS SINNER. THINK FUNKY THOUGHTS AND IN THE NAME OF THE REVEREND FLEA SING, "GIVE IT AWAY, GIVE IT AWAY, NOW!"

Dear Reverend Groove,
I have a dark secret. I have been listening to Meatloaf on my Ghettoblaster. I bought his tape and stuck a "Really Funky Sounds" sticker over the Meatloaf label. Can I be saved?
                  Signed Sad Suzie.

**WELL SISTER, I NOTICE YOU DIDN'T SEND A DONATION TO SAVE CREATION FROM THE WRATH OF RADIO-FRIENDLY-ROCK! AS GRAND MASTER OF THE GHETTOBLASTER, I URGE YOU TO SEND ₤200 TO THE CHURCH OF FUNK. AND YOUR PENANCE MY PRIMO SISTER IS TO LISTEN TO THE FUNKY MELODIES OF FUNKADELIC AND THE GROOVACIOUS GROOVES OF THE FRENCH FUNK FEDERATION, FOR THREE MONTHS, TWENTY FOUR HOURS A DAY TO TRY AND GET YOUR FUNKY FEET BACK ON THE GROOVE STREET OF LIFE.
LET ME HEAR YOU SAY "HUUUH!"**

Dear Rev. Groove,
    I'm getting married soon, but I can't decide between Sly and the Family Stone, "Family Affair" or The Brothers Johnston, "Get the funk out ma face" as our wedding song whilst we walk up the aisle.
           Can you help Reverend Groove?

**OH LORDY YESSSSS! IT'S A TIME TO TIE THE LOVE KNOT, BUT IT'S ALSO TIME FOR SOME FUNKY GUIDANCE FROM YOURS TRULY. FOR A SMALL DONATION OF ₤100 OR MORE, I'LL GIVE YOU SOME FREE ADVICE. FOR A WEDDING MADE IN FUNK HEAVEN YOU GOTTA TIE THE KNOT WHILE YOU TROT TO THE HOT, HOT, HOT SOULFUL SOUNDS OF ST. JAMES BROWN'S, "I GOT YOU!" FOR THAT IS THE SONG FOR THE UNITED FOUNDATION OF FUNKY BROTHERS AND SOUL SISTERS OF TOGETHERNESS. THE VERY REVEREND T GROOVE WANTS YOUR MONEY TO SAVE YOUR SOULS. YOU GOTTA "GIVE IT AWAY, GIVE IT AWAY, NOW!" SO SEND YOUR MONEY SINNERS, TO THE SEVENTH ZOGIAN CHURCH OF FUNK, TODAY.
MAY THE FUNK BE WITH YOU!**

ZAG's GUIDE TO... HOW TO KEEP YOUR

YOU MIGHT THINK THAT GOING OUT WITH SUPERMODELS IS BLOOMIN' EASY... WELL, IT'S NOT!
SO MANY SUPER STAR HUNKS ARE VYING FOR SO FEW SUPERMODELS.
IT'S UP TO YOU TO BE A SUPERMODEL SWEETIE!!
AND BY GEORGE-UPON-AVON, HAVE I GOT SOME SUPER HINTS FOR YOU!

READ ON...

CHAPTER ONE: The Meeting:

SO YOU JUST HAPPEN TO BUMP INTO LINDA EVANGELISTA AT YOUR LOCAL CAR BOOT SALE, AND EXCHANGE PHONE NUMBERS. YOU'RE DASHING HOME IN YOUR FIAT PANDA TO TELL ALL YOUR MATES OF YOUR GOOD FORTUNE!
WELL, STOP RIGHT THERE YOUNG LADDY-ME-JACK. BEFORE YOU MAKE AN UTTER DECKCHAIR OF YOURSELF, THERE ARE SOME THINGS THAT NEED A DOIN'!
AND CHAPTER TWO HAS THE ANSWERS!

CHAPTER TWO: The Motor:

THE FIRST QUESTION YOU MUST ASK YOURSELF IS "Do I have a Ferarri?" IF THE ANSWER IS "NO" AND YOU'VE GOT NO MONEY, THEN BORROW £100 AND NIP DOWN TO YOUR LOCAL MOTOR SHOP AND BUY A "PANDARRI" KIT FROM ZAG REV (Sporting kits for Gentlemen!) WHICH WILL TRANSFORM YOUR PATHETIC FIAT PANDA INTO A FAB-TASTIC FERARRI LOOKALIKE IN UNDER TWO MINUTES!

Lots of love Cindy

miss you much! Naomi xx

Call me, Kate

miss you mr. sexy trousers, love Linda xx

BIG KISSES Ru Paul

SUPERMODEL, SUPER!

CHAPTER THREE: The Bait:

THE SECOND QUESTION YOU MUST ASK YOURSELF IS "How on earth can I keep my Supermodel entertained?"

WELL, IF THERE ISN'T MUCH 'ROUND YOUR WAY TO KEEP AN INTERNATIONAL BEAUTY INTERESTED, THEN IT'S UP TO YOU TO TEMPT HER.. OTHERWISE YOUR PRECIOUS NAOMI OR HELENA WILL BE OFF TO MILAN LIKE A HOT SNOT!

THAT'S WHY YOU MUST BUY THE PATENTED "ZAGGY-WALK CATWALK".

"OH, DARLING, J.P GAULTIER JUST RANG. HE WANTS ME TO FLY TO PARIS TO DO A FASHION SHOW!"

"OH, DON'T BOTHER WITH THAT! I'LL RING BARRY AND THE LADS AND GET THEM TO COME OVER. I'VE GOT A "ZAGGY-WALK" IN THE BACK GARDEN, WHY NOT PUT ON A SHOW FOR US, LUV?"

SO, SHE LIKES YOUR CAR, SHE'S THRILLED WITH YOUR ZAGGYWALK.
BUT, IS SHE REALLY HAPPY?
HOW CAN I GET HER TO STAY FOREVER?

CHAPTER FOUR: The Hook, Line and Sinker:

IF YOU WANT TO KEEP YOUR SUPERMODEL-SUPER-HAPPY, YOU'VE GOT TO BE A SUPER-SOPPY-GUY!
SIMPLY FEED HER SOME OF THESE TRIED AND TESTED ZAG LOVE LINES AND YOUR SUPER-GAL WILL BE SUPER-IMPRESSED!

"Your loveliness blossoms like a smouldering peach!"

"Could that scent be a million white roses mixed with Himalayan mountain dew... no, it's just you my darling!"

"I feel like a nymph sauntering through a Candyfloss cloud when I steal a kiss from you, my gentle love dove!"

ZAG'S BOOK: "MY LIFE AS A CATWALK CUPID" IS AVAILABLE FROM ZOG BOOKS, PO BOX 75 FOR JUST £75.00

ZIG'S CELEBRITY CEREAL LOOKALIKES

Here's Lenny Henry with a perm

OO-ER CINDY CORNFLAKE

CORN POPS

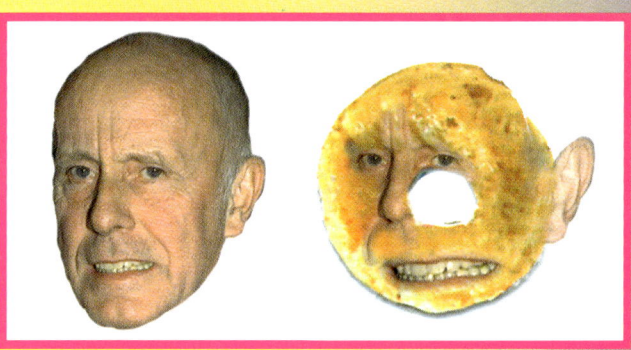
I don't believe it! It's Victor Meldrew

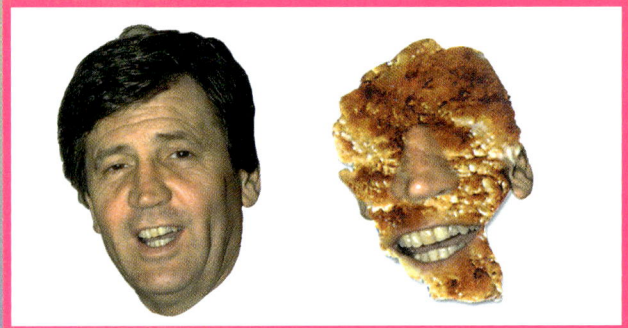
It's Melvin Bran from the South Bran Show

FRUIT AND FIBRE!

ALL BRAN

I don't have a Barry Gibb cereal lookalike, but here he is anyway.

ZIG AND ZAG'S GUIDE TO HOW TO HAVE CHRISTMAS ANY DAY YOU WANT!

INGREDIENTS:

Ice, popcorn, bubble bath, flour, a red dress, a red hat, a cushion, dad's black boots, a sack, old toys, a piece of wood, toilet roll inserts, your teddy bears, a stuffed toy cat, next door's dog, lots of lights, an electric fan, a flower pot, a ballerina dress, a wig, cotton wool, a carrot, two twigs, a ladder, the phone number for the fire station, tin foil, and no parents at home!

"THEN, YOU MIX ALL THE INGREDIENTS TOGETHER AND YOU'LL HAVE THE PERFECT CHRISTMAS..."

"INDEED! HAVE A LOOK AT THE NEXT PAGE AND SEE FOR YOURSELF!"

KNIT A YIBBLE SWEATER
for your man
EXCLUSIVELY from

FREE

PEGLOR GIFTS

You can knit this smashing sweater all by yourself. Peglor the Almighty, Ruler of all Universes, has decreed that you be given this exclusive

"Zig and Zag knitting pattern" ABSOLUTELY FREE!

Now, all you need is 135 balls of hand-loomed Yibble fur, available only from Peglor's Yibble Farm at the Castle of the Impaler.

59 yibbles

76 yibbles

N.B: For any creature lovers out there who feel sorry for the thousands of naked Yibbles who will be facing a harsh winter without their fur, we at PEGLOR GIFTS would like to point out that whilst Yibbles are indeed peaceful, harmless creatures, they do have dire table manners! So we don't feel guilty about shaving them and making jumpers out their fur! So there!

Send an S.A.E for details to: **PEGLOR GIFTS, Castle of the Impaler, Planet Destructo.**

Zig's Anorak World

The History of the Anorak

In the 17th Century, Anne of the Rack decided to make a coat with a convenient hood on it, that kept out the rain...

...naturally, she was accused of witchcraft for not getting her hair wet. And so she was sentenced to death.

She narrowly escaped the executioners blade when he chopped her hood off instead of her head. Then she escaped by using the hood as a parachute...

"Nice hood Robin!"

ANORAKS 'R US

After many years in hiding she opened a shop in the woods to show others her wonderous creation...and thus the Ann-o-rak was born.

HERE'S THE ULTIMATE GUIDE TO WHAT ANORAKS ARE AVAILABLE TODAY!

GENUINE PSYCHO POWDERED SHARKS

Have your own KILLER SHARK POOL!

THE REAL THING, JUST ADD WATER!

Delivered to your own home.
Watch them eat your friends.
Not sold to children under 6 years.

FREE SHARK TANK
with every shark family sold
plus *'Shark Attack'* magazine-everything
you ever wanted to know about sharks.

SEND Ƶ3.95 per Shark.
Ƶ6.50 for Two. Ƶ19.95 for the Family.

📞 PHONE FOR CATALOGUE.

AMAZING
DEAD ANIMALS DELIVERED DIRECT.

These natural sun dried animals make ideal gifts for everyone.
All animals are guaranteed dead before we **kill them!**

Free as a very special gift, you can have our beautiful viewing atriums-view your dead animal from every angle.

STOP PRESS! Ming Pandas, just in time before extinction.

📞 Dial Dead Animals Direct 0①③⑧-DEAD

GHOST IN A CAN

Scare the Pants off your Friends.

It's the spookiest suprise they'll ever get.
These innocent cans contain a giant life like ...

65 FOOT HOVERING GHOST!

Made from sturdy 100% polychlorideflamaline.
Available in 3 colours dead green, swamp grey, guts pink.

SEND CASH NOW ➔ ✉

☢ Toxic Waste Disposals Ltd.
Box no. 4975 Zog.

ADOPT ♥ GAVIN

☺ Just look at this happy chap.

But there's saddness behind his smile, you could give Gavin a new life.
Here's your chance to adopt Gavin for a limited period only!

YOU CAN ADOPT GAVIN FOR ONLY . . . . Ƶ69.95 PER WEEK.

He's guaranteed to bring warmth and happiness into your mundane lives. Gavin comes with his own paddling pool. Watch him splash away the hours.

✍ Write to: ADOPT GAVIN,
P.O. Box 8843,
New Guinea.

POWER SHOES from QVC
HEY YOU!

Be an Olympic runner with these scientifically designed power shoes. They're faster due to our patented real

ANIMAL FEET SOLES.

That's right, we trapped some of the fastest animals in the world just for you! With the help of genetic photocopying we've reproduced natures fastest feet onto these fantastic shoes.
So send this order form now and recieve a free copy of "100 great steam trains" FREE

ORDER NOW!

- 1 pair Ƶ9.95 ☐
- 2 pairs Ƶ17.95 ☐

Name: _____
Address: _____

QVC POWER SHOES: 0 ①③⑧ - paws. Have your credit card no. ready!

MAKE A MILLION ZOGABUCKS

READ THIS BOOK
BE INSTANTLY RICH!

Send Ƶ500.00 to Zag,
10 Zogland Heights, Planet Zog.

boring small print, not worth reading.
non-refundable ... and we're not saying
who'll be the millionare!

☎ PHONE THE RODLINE

A date with Gavin's brother Rodrigez.
WINE, DANCING, OPERA, ROMANCE
GUARANTEED L'AMOUR.

CALL THE RODLINE NOW.

Dial 000351-56221 now!
Calls cost Ƶ89.00 per minute.

Free complimentary cheese platter on confirmation of first date.

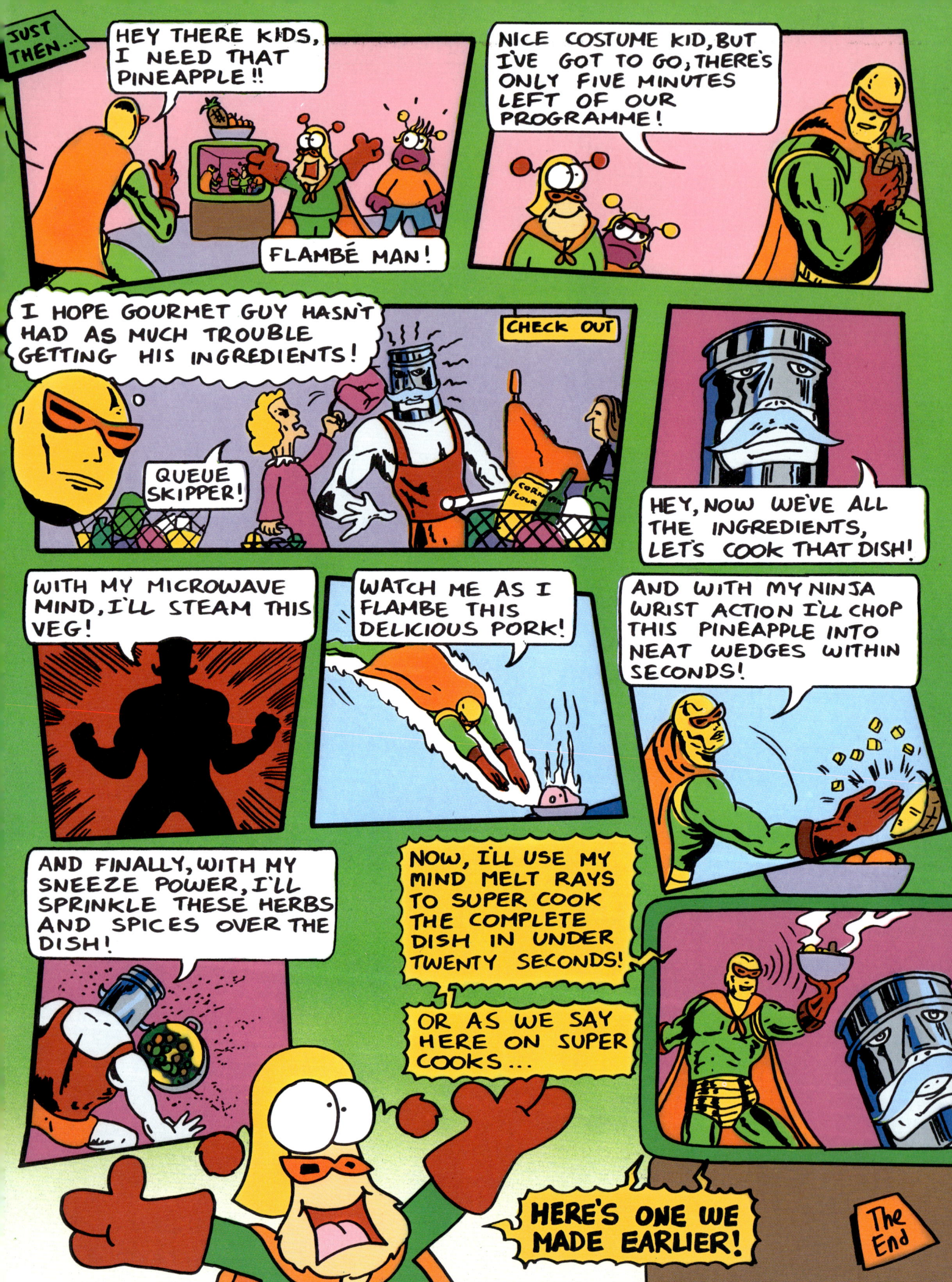

INTERPLANETRY ITINERARY

DAY ONE

AFTER A LIGHT BUFFET OF LIVE WEEBLES, WE'LL HAVE A MEET AND GREET SESSION AT THE PALACE OF THE IMPALER WITH OUR PEGLOR TOURS REPRESENTATIVE, DORIS, TO SWAP IDEAS ON PILLAGING AND MERCILESS DESTRUCTION. THEN IT'S ALL ABOARD THE GOOD SHIP "PULVERISE 2" FOR THE FUN TO BEGIN.

FIRST STOP IS THE PLANET ENTLE, WHERE YOU CAN STROLL THROUGH THE CHARMING NARROW STREETS AND HANGING GARDENS OF THE LITTLE ENTLIAN VILLAGES, SEE THE GENTLE DOE-EYED ENTLE FOLK AT PLAY OR GAZE UPON THE WONDROUS WATERFALL OF ETERNAL PEACE.

THEN AT NOON IT'S TIME TO GRAB YOUR PULVER STICKS AND GET SET FOR A FUN COMPETITION; "VILLAGE DESTRUCTION," SEE IF YOU CAN MATCH PEGLOR'S HIGH SCORE OF 2000 POINTS. YOU GET 20 POINTS FOR AN ENTIRE VILLAGE AND 500 POINTS BONUS FOR THE TOTAL DESTRUCTION OF THE WATERFALL! AT 2.30PM IT'S BARBECUED ENTLIANS, CAJUN STYLE!

DAY TWO

AFTER A SHORT FLIGHT, WE BUZZ BOMB AND ANNIHILATE SOME OF THE MOST CHARMING AND PICTURESQUE, INHABITED MOONS YOU'LL SEE IN ANY GALAXY.
AND FOR LUNCH, YOU'LL BE INVITED TO FEAST ON A PLANET OF YOUR CHOICE FROM OUR FABULOUS PLANET BUFFET.

DAY THREE

IF YOU'RE NOT TOO TIRED BRINGING MISERY AND MINDLESS OBLIVION TO THE WEAKER PLANETS OF OUR GALAXIES, THEN HOP ON BOARD TODAY'S OPTIONAL EXCURSION; TO THE WARRING PLANETS OF K-7 AND UKAR, WHERE DEATH AND DESTRUCTION ARE EVERYDAY SIGHTS. DON'T FORGET YOUR CAMERA FOR SOME EXCELLENT PHOTO OPPORTUNITIES.

DAY FOUR

PUT A FAMILY OF YOUR CHOICE OUT OF THEIR HOME IN OUR FUN GAME, "SEND 'EM PACKIN'."

THEN RITUALLY DESTROY THEIR HOME OR KEEP IT AS A SOUVENIR TO BRING HOME TO THE KIDS.

THEN JUST BEFORE WE GO HOME, WE DO OUR BIT FOR INTER-PLANETARY PEACE, BY BLOWING BOTH PLANETS INTO KINGDOM COME! WELL, THEY WON'T BE FIGHTING ANYMORE, NOW WILL THEY?

DAY FIVE

PEGLOR'S SURPRISE TRIP TO A PLANET CALLED EARTH. IT'S GONNA BE ONE HOT DAY OF DESTRUCTION, THAT'S ALL WE'RE GOING TO SAY. BUT DON'T FORGET YOUR PULVER STICKS!

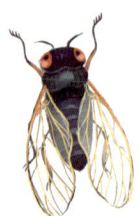

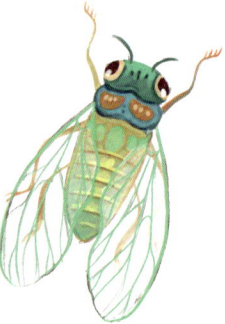

Cicada City

a Bug Club story

written by Gina Gallois   illustrated by Elisabeth Clover

For my sweetie bird and my baby bee,
with much gratitude to Fab,
and all those who have believed in and supported this project.

Special thanks to Kirstynn Joseph and Caroline King
for excellence in fact checking.

Published by Moonflower Press, 2021

Copyright © 2021 by Gina Gallois and Moonflower Press.

Printed in China.

Book design by Melissa Bailey.
Edited by Lor Bingham.

All rights reserved. This book or any portion thereof may not be reproduced or used in any manner whatsoever without the express written permission of the publisher except for the use of brief quotations in a book review.

Library of Congress Control Number: 2020946127
ISBN-13: 978-1-954322-22-6 Hardback
ISBN-13: 978-1-954322-23-3 Paperback
ISBN-13: 978-1-954322-24-0 Ebook

For permission requests, contact Moonflower Press at Moonflowerpress.com

Meet the Bug Club members!

Hyacinth

Looks closely and photographs all the bugs.

Jaylen

Cares for the critter keeper and butterfly net.

Sakura

Records their findings in the Bug Club Journal.

"Fly away, ladybugs! It's been a pleasure watching you grow," says Hyacinth, as they take flight.
"Which bugs should we look for next?" Jaylen asks.
"Cicadas are next on the list," Sakura replies.

BROOD X

Brood X, one of the largest groups of 17-year cicada nymphs, emerged in parts of the United States in 2021 and in 2004 before that.

They are known as **periodical cicadas** because a new generation emerges every 13 or 17 years. There are 12 different broods of 17-year cicadas and three broods of 13-year cicadas.

"Are we ready? Magnifying glass and camera, check," says Hyacinth.

"Critter keeper and butterfly net, check," Jaylen confirms.

"Insect guide and Bug Club Journal, check," says Sakura. "Let's go."

Cicadas spend most of their lives underground as **nymphs**.

18 inches

After **hatching**, they fall to the ground and burrow into the earth, to a depth of about six to 20 inches, (15-50 cm.) Underground, cicada nymphs do NOT sleep for 17 years! They use their strong front legs to dig and excavate chambers near roots where they feed on xylem sap and grow. Finally, they emerge, shed their outer shell, dry out for several days, and fly off to look for a mate.

The Bug Club members, Hyacinth, Jaylen, and Sakura, are also neighbors and best friends. They meet every Saturday, rain or shine.

This Saturday is a beautiful, warm, sunny day in May. Summer is approaching.

In their quest for cicadas, the friends creep carefully around flower beds and between bushes.

Cicadas **emerge** when the ground temperature reaches about 65°F (18°C,) usually beginning in late April to early June, as far north as New York State and as far south as Georgia, from New England in the east, to Illinois in the west. In order to emerge on time, periodical cicadas count the seasonal pulses of fluid flowing in the roots from which they feed. After 13 or 17 years, the warming of the soil is their signal to return to the surface and take to the skies.

"Hey, look!" Jaylen yells, pointing to a creature wiggling wildly on a tree.

"Wow! Incredible!" Hyacinth marvels.

"It's a molting cicada!" squeals Sakura.

Cicada shells are called **exuviae**.

The process of shedding the outer shell is called **molting**. Once a cicada sheds its shell, it takes five to six days for its exoskeleton to dry and harden enough to mate.

Brood X cicadas are black with clear wings and normally have red eyes. Annual cicadas are seen every year and are green and black in color.

As the cicada wiggles and waggles out of its shell, its wings unfurl, becoming see-through as they dry.

"Amazing..." Hyacinth sighs.

"That one is singing! Only the male cicadas sing. He's calling a mate," Sakura says.

"Should we catch him before he flies away?" asks Jaylen nervously.

"No!" the girls shout. Jaylen looks relieved.

"We can't keep him from finding a mate. We can keep his shell, though. He doesn't need it anymore," Sakura reasons.

Cicada song is the loudest insect sound known to humans – as loud as a rock concert! Male cicadas use organs called **tymbals** to produce surprisingly loud buzzing noises like a stick scraping repeatedly over a ribbed surface. Each species has their own distinct sounds, and the males make a variety of sounds: a mating call, a distress call, an encounter call, etc... Female cicadas do not sing, but respond by clicking their wings.

"What should we name him?" Sakura wonders.
"Let's call him Cid the Cicada," Jaylen says.
"Good luck, Cid!" they all call after him as he takes off. Jaylen puts Cid's shell in the critter keeper.

Some scientists think cicadas may have evolved to **emerge** on an unpredictable schedule and in such large numbers that some would **escape predators** to reproduce. Another theory is that these long periods underground helped them **survive climate extremes**. However, no one knows for sure.

"What did Cid do underground for 17 years?" Hyacinth wonders.

"He worked in a subterranean scientific laboratory," Jaylen imagines.

"And after work, he sipped root sap smoothies and watched TV," Hyacinth giggles.

"We could be walking around on top of a whole cicada civilization!" Sakura says.

The kids find so many cicada shells, the critter keeper is soon overflowing. The gang heads back to Sakura's house for a snack and to plan their next meeting.

"Let's build an aboveground cicada city for the shells we found," Jaylen suggests.

"That's a great idea!" the girls agree.

Female cicadas lay their **eggs** in slits they cut into the thin branches of trees and shrubs. When the eggs hatch, tiny nymphs the size of an ant fall to the ground, burrow, and return to the surface one, 13 or 17 years later. Nymphs require a solid, safe place such as a tree trunk to emerge from their shells and stay for several days as their exoskeleton hardens so they can mate. A few **stragglers** may also emerge one to four years early or late.

The next week, the Bug Club meets at Jaylen's house.

"I'm going to build houses with bunk beds stacked 10 high," Hyacinth says excitedly.

"I'll make a school with the best cicada playground ever!" Sakura exclaims. "We are going to have so much fun!"

"I'll build a theater, with curtains, balconies, and tiny costumes," Jaylen says. "Let's keep collecting shells. Cicada City needs more residents."

A mature cicada's **life span** is only two to six weeks. In that time, they mate and females lay eggs. The eggs hatch after six to 10 weeks and the tiny nymphs fall to the ground to burrow.

"We collected 167 cicada shells. Not bad for one week," Sakura says, nodding at her notebook approvingly.

"There should be trillions of 17-year cicadas from Brood X this summer," Hyacinth says.

Jaylen, ready to get started, says enthusiastically, "Let's get these little critters settled in their new homes."

"I'll take pictures and my parents can help me post them online," Hyacinth says.

In some places, there can be as many as 1.5 million per acre, bringing the total **Brood X population** into the trillions.

In no time, the Bug Club's social media accounts start trending. Cicada City goes viral!

Food-loving cicadas show off their baking skills. Creative cicadas share their paintings. Sporty cicadas post selfies from their latest triathlon.

The kids' parents help them post videos of the cicadas performing daring stunts on tiny motorcycles, and stand-up comedy routines.

While the sky buzzes with cicada song, social media is abuzz with cicada mania.

The Bug Club, now famous, hosts a Cicada City Open House in Jaylen's backyard.

The open house is in full swing when a news van rolls up and a reporter interviews the Bug Club for the evening news.
  Cicada mania is at fever pitch by midsummer.

Then one Saturday, Jaylen looks around and asks, "Is it me, or have the cicadas been quieter lately?"

"I think you're right," Sakura admits sadly. "Cicada season is coming to an end."

Cicada season typically lasts from late April until mid-July, depending on the weather and when the soil reaches the proper temperature.

"Will we have to wait 17 years to see them again?" asks Jaylen.

"Nope! Don't worry - annual cicadas come out every year," Hyacinth answers.

The next generation of **Brood X will return in 2038**. Seventeen-year cicadas from Brood XIII are due in 2024 and Brood XIV is due in 2025. Also in 2025, 13-year cicadas from Brood XIX are expected to emerge.

"What kind of bugs should we look for next week?" asks Sakura.

Hyacinth, looking dreamy, asks, "What if we held next week's meeting at **night**?"

"To look for moths?" Jaylen asks hopefully.

"Exactly!"

The size of the yearly cicada population can influence the populations of their predators, such as birds, fish, and small mammals, who may then produce more offspring. The bodies of decaying cicadas also provide an important source of nitrogen for growing trees. The **cycle of life** continues.

My Bug Club Notes

Write or draw your own insect observations here.